this journal belongs

to:

What is the subconscious mind?

The subconscious mind refers to a part of our mind that exists below conscious awareness. It is responsible for storing and processing information that we may not be aware of in our conscious mind but still influences our thoughts, emotions, and behaviors.

The subconscious mind plays a crucial role in shaping our beliefs, habits, and automatic responses. It is believed to hold memories, experiences, and emotions that may have been forgotten or repressed. These stored experiences and emotions can influence our perceptions, attitudes, and decision-making processes.

The subconscious mind also plays a role in processing and interpreting sensory information. It helps us make sense of the world around us by filtering and organizing incoming information based on our existing beliefs and experiences.

What is subconscious programming?

Subconscious programming refers to how our subconscious mind absorbs and stores information, beliefs, and behaviors that shape our thoughts, emotions, and actions. Our programming happens mostly during early childhood when our minds are highly impressionable. Through interactions with our environment, such as family, culture, education, and experiences, our subconscious mind absorbs and internalizes these influences, forming the foundation of our belief systems and automatic responses. Because our subconscious programming operates beneath our conscious awareness, it acts as a filter through which we interpret and respond to the world around us.

Looking at it through a Human Design lens, our subconscious programming is essentially the conditioning (a.k.a. societal/familial messages and beliefs) that was repeated enough when we were open and vulnerable enough to accept it as truth, whether we are consciously aware of it or not.

This happens mostly when we are younger — children ages 0-7 are particularly susceptible— but in my experience, this openness extends, to a degree, through adolescence and into our 20s. It can also happen when we are in a vulnerable state—scared, unsure, in a new place, under duress or control of another person, etc. For example, this is how cults "brainwash" their participants—by programming them with beliefs when they are in a vulnerable state.

Our subconscious programming can be both beneficial and limiting. It can support our growth and success if it aligns with our goals and desires, but it can also hold us back if it includes negative or self-limiting beliefs. We might unknowingly not pursue something because we watched someone in our family fail at something similar, even if our situation is completely different. We might discredit a talent or hobby because we were told it was not worthwhile growing up. We might not be open to connecting with someone based on superficial impressions because we were told to believe something about another person's looks, abilities, race, class, or gender.

How does subconscious reprogramming work?

Subconscious reprogramming intentionally modifies the deeply ingrained beliefs, thought patterns, and behaviors stored in our subconscious. It involves identifying these limiting beliefs (or simply identifying their undesirable repercussions) and replacing them with empowering ones through affirmations, visualization, hypnosis, and meditation.

How do certain beliefs or ideas make their way to the subconscious? After all, we have a conscious mind that can filter out stimuli and messages. How do we access the beliefs cemented when we were younger now that we have developed more critical thinking? Won't our conscious minds fight back?

Well, the key lies in:

1. **Communicating with the subconscious** in a language that it understands, like emotion, images, and symbols

2. **Repetition**— by actively engaging in this process, we can transform our subconscious programming, align it with our goals and desires, and see the results we want in our lives.

How to use this journal

The process of using this journal is simple—there are two different spreads: daily and weekly.

Daily spread:

The daily spread is designed to be a check-in each day (or a few times a week) to align your mind with where your energy is going. You can do this any time during the day. What is important is that it feels energizing and helpful for you.

Here is a breakdown on how each question is intended to be used:

Today, I feel energized by...

This is where you can reflect on what you're feeling motivated to do or excited about. This could be an activity that you already have planned/already did or something you'd like to make time for.

It could also be something simple like enjoying the weather, taking a walk, or cooking a meal.

 Today, I feel drained or frustrated by...

This is an opportunity to note any friction, frustration, dread, or low energy you felt throughout the day and think about where it might have come from.

When something is frustrating or not feeling good, it can be an indicator that we could do it differently to align better with our life force energy.

 A desire I have, or a frustration I would like to shift, is...

What change do you want to make in your life? This is where you state the reality that you want to experience. If it's something small, you might notice fast results and move on to a new desire. If it's something bigger that will take more time to materialize, you may repeat the same desire for months (or longer).

An affirmation (or multiple) to describe my desired reality is...

Next, write some affirmations to help communicate your desire to your subconscious mind. When we affirm a reality, we want to make sure we're doing it in the positive. Instead of saying "I don't want debt," we would say "I have a 0 balance on all my credit cards." Otherwise, your subconscious hears "debt" and will focus on the concept of debt.

If you desire something more general, like a feeling or state of being, it's good to use "I AM [insert feeling/situation/state you want to embody]."

If you're creating something more tangible, like the debt example, affirm your desire as if it has already happened—"My credit cards have all been paid in full and have 0 balance."

Remember: you do not have to be super specific in your desire if that does not feel right to you. Wanting to be in a certain state or feel a certain feeling is fully valid.

Anytime something in this process feels off or frustrating to you, just do it in a way that feels good! There are no rules.

 I feel grateful for...

List a few things you are grateful for. When we express gratitude, we are training our subconscious mind to look for positive outcomes in the world.

Weekly spread:

The weekly spread is an opportunity to reflect weekly (or a few times a month) so you can notice patterns in what is energizing you, frustrating you, and the progress you've made in your subconscious reprogramming.

Just by being aware of any patterns or progress, you can begin to make different choices and target these areas in your daily exercises.

 Looking at the last few entries, what consistently energized or excited me? How can I made more space for those things in my life?

 *What consistently drained me?
How could I minimize these activities?*

 Have I had any negative thoughts or frustrations? What new thoughts would help support the reality I want to create?

 What shifts have I noticed in my thinking or reality since I began reprogramming my mind?

DAILY & WEEKLY REFLECTION PAGES

date: _____

Today, I feel energized by...

Today, I feel drained or frustrated by...

A desire I have, or a frustration I would like to shift, is...

An affirmation (or multiple) to describe my desired reality is...

I feel grateful for...

date: _____

Today, I feel energized by...

Today, I feel drained or frustrated by...

A desire I have, or a frustration I would like to shift, is...

An affirmation (or multiple) to describe my desired reality is...

I feel grateful for...

date: _____

Today, I feel energized by...

Today, I feel drained or frustrated by...

A desire I have, or a frustration I would like to shift, is...

An affirmation (or multiple) to describe my desired reality is...

I feel grateful for...

date: _____

Today, I feel energized by...

Today, I feel drained or frustrated by...

A desire I have, or a frustration I would like to shift, is...

An affirmation (or multiple) to describe my desired reality is...

I feel grateful for...

date: _____

Today, I feel energized by...

Today, I feel drained or frustrated by...

A desire I have, or a frustration I would like to shift, is...

An affirmation (or multiple) to describe my desired reality is...

I feel grateful for...

date: _____

Today, I feel energized by...

Today, I feel drained or frustrated by...

A desire I have, or a frustration I would like to shift, is...

An affirmation (or multiple) to describe my desired reality is...

I feel grateful for...

date: _____

Looking at the last few entries, what consistently energized or excited me? How can I made more space for those things in my life?

*What consistently drained me?
How could I minimize these activities?*

Have I had any negative thoughts or frustrations? How could I shift these thoughts to match the reality I want to create?

What changes have I noticed in my thinking or reality since I began reprogramming my mind?

this week, I felt energized...

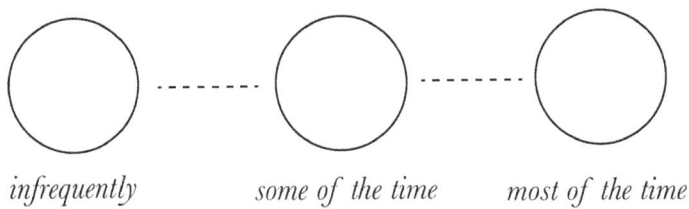

i felt positive about reaching my goals and making my dreams reality...

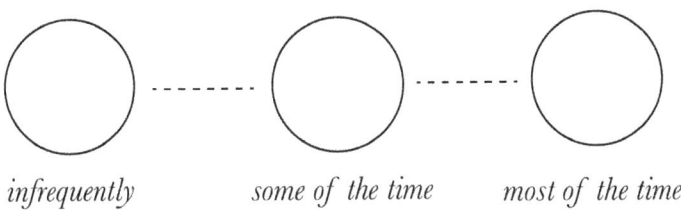

i felt magnetic, flowing, and satisfied...

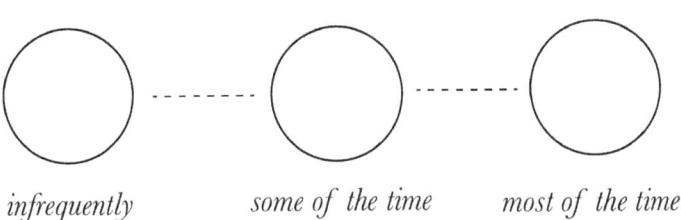

I have a magnetic aura.

date: _____

Today, I feel energized by...

Today, I feel drained or frustrated by...

A desire I have, or a frustration I would like to shift, is...

An affirmation (or multiple) to describe my desired reality is...

I feel grateful for...

date: _____

Today, I feel energized by...

Today, I feel drained or frustrated by...

A desire I have, or a frustration I would like to shift, is...

An affirmation (or multiple) to describe my desired reality is...

I feel grateful for...

date: _____

Today, I feel energized by...

Today, I feel drained or frustrated by...

A desire I have, or a frustration I would like to shift, is...

An affirmation (or multiple) to describe my desired reality is...

I feel grateful for...

date: _____

Today, I feel energized by...

Today, I feel drained or frustrated by...

A desire I have, or a frustration I would like to shift, is...

An affirmation (or multiple) to describe my desired reality is...

I feel grateful for...

date: _____

Today, I feel energized by...

Today, I feel drained or frustrated by...

A desire I have, or a frustration I would like to shift, is...

An affirmation (or multiple) to describe my desired reality is...

I feel grateful for...

date: _____

Today, I feel energized by...

Today, I feel drained or frustrated by...

A desire I have, or a frustration I would like to shift, is...

An affirmation (or multiple) to describe my desired reality is...

I feel grateful for...

The world needs what I have to offer.

date: _____

Looking at the last few entries, what consistently energized or excited me? How can I made more space for those things in my life?

*What consistently drained me?
How could I minimize these activities?*

Have I had any negative thoughts or frustrations? How could I shift these thoughts to match the reality I want to create?

What changes have I noticed in my thinking or reality since I began reprogramming my mind?

this week, I felt energized...

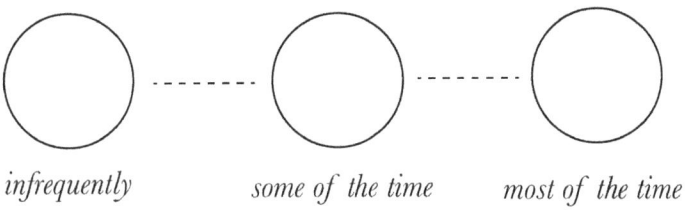

i felt positive about reaching my goals and making my dreams reality...

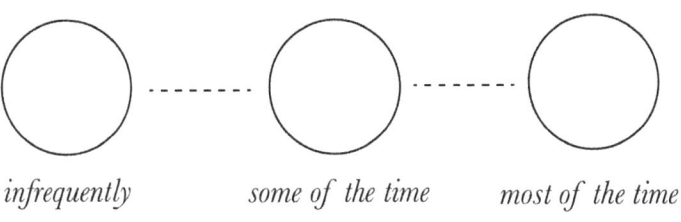

i felt magnetic, flowing, and satisfied...

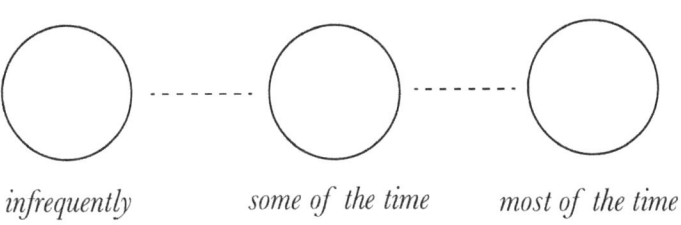

date: _____

Today, I feel energized by...

Today, I feel drained or frustrated by...

A desire I have, or a frustration I would like to shift, is...

An affirmation (or multiple) to describe my desired reality is...

I feel grateful for...

date: _____

Today, I feel energized by...

Today, I feel drained or frustrated by...

A desire I have, or a frustration I would like to shift, is...

An affirmation (or multiple) to describe my desired reality is...

I feel grateful for...

date: _____

Today, I feel energized by...

Today, I feel drained or frustrated by...

A desire I have, or a frustration I would like to shift, is...

An affirmation (or multiple) to describe my desired reality is...

I feel grateful for...

date: _____

Today, I feel energized by...

Today, I feel drained or frustrated by...

A desire I have, or a frustration I would like to shift, is...

An affirmation (or multiple) to describe my desired reality is...

I feel grateful for...

date: _____

Today, I feel energized by...

Today, I feel drained or frustrated by...

A desire I have, or a frustration I would like to shift, is...

An affirmation (or multiple) to describe my desired reality is...

I feel grateful for...

date: _____

Today, I feel energized by...

Today, I feel drained or frustrated by...

A desire I have, or a frustration I would like to shift, is...

An affirmation (or multiple) to describe my desired reality is...

I feel grateful for...

date: _____

Looking at the last few entries, what consistently energized or excited me? How can I made more space for those things in my life?

*What consistently drained me?
How could I minimize these activities?*

Have I had any negative thoughts or frustrations? How could I shift these thoughts to match the reality I want to create?

What changes have I noticed in my thinking or reality since I began reprogramming my mind?

this week, I felt energized...

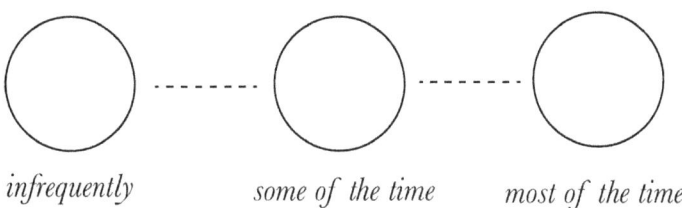

i felt positive about reaching my goals and making my dreams reality...

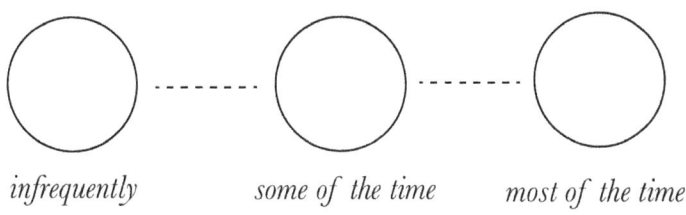

i felt magnetic, flowing, and satisfied...

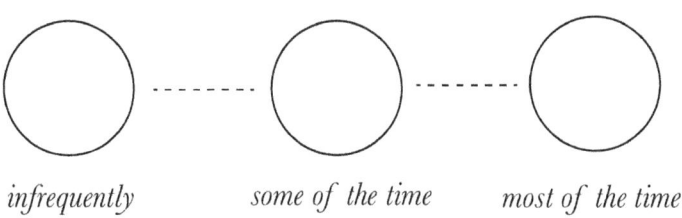

It is safe to leave space in my life for new things.

date: _____

Today, I feel energized by...

Today, I feel drained or frustrated by...

A desire I have, or a frustration I would like to shift, is...

An affirmation (or multiple) to describe my desired reality is...

I feel grateful for...

date: _____

Today, I feel energized by...

Today, I feel drained or frustrated by...

A desire I have, or a frustration I would like to shift, is...

An affirmation (or multiple) to describe my desired reality is...

I feel grateful for...

date: _____

Today, I feel energized by...

Today, I feel drained or frustrated by...

A desire I have, or a frustration I would like to shift, is...

An affirmation (or multiple) to describe my desired reality is...

I feel grateful for...

date: _____

Today, I feel energized by...

Today, I feel drained or frustrated by...

A desire I have, or a frustration I would like to shift, is...

An affirmation (or multiple) to describe my desired reality is...

I feel grateful for...

date: _____

Today, I feel energized by...

Today, I feel drained or frustrated by...

A desire I have, or a frustration I would like to shift, is...

An affirmation (or multiple) to describe my desired reality is...

I feel grateful for...

date: _____

Today, I feel energized by...

Today, I feel drained or frustrated by...

A desire I have, or a frustration I would like to shift, is...

An affirmation (or multiple) to describe my desired reality is...

I feel grateful for...

I am willing to experience satisfaction daily.

date: _____

Looking at the last few entries, what consistently energized or excited me? How can I made more space for those things in my life?

*What consistently drained me?
How could I minimize these activities?*

Have I had any negative thoughts or frustrations? How could I shift these thoughts to match the reality I want to create?

What changes have I noticed in my thinking or reality since I began reprogramming my mind?

this week, I felt energized...

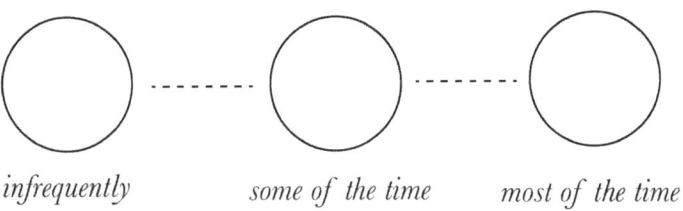

i felt positive about reaching my goals and making my dreams reality...

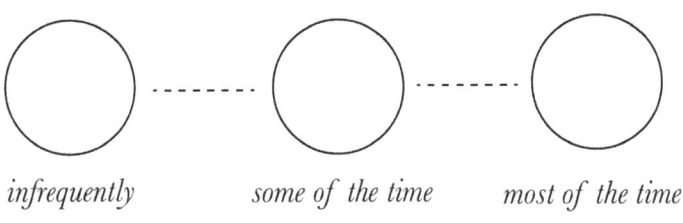

i felt magnetic, flowing, and satisfied...

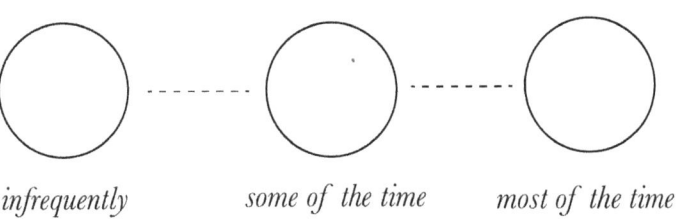

date: _____

Today, I feel energized by...

Today, I feel drained or frustrated by...

A desire I have, or a frustration I would like to shift, is...

An affirmation (or multiple) to describe my desired reality is...

I feel grateful for...

date:  _____

Today, I feel energized by...

Today, I feel drained or frustrated by...

A desire I have, or a frustration I would like to shift, is...

An affirmation (or multiple) to describe my desired reality is...

I feel grateful for...

date: _____

Today, I feel energized by...

Today, I feel drained or frustrated by...

A desire I have, or a frustration I would like to shift, is...

An affirmation (or multiple) to describe my desired reality is...

I feel grateful for...

date: _____

Today, I feel energized by...

Today, I feel drained or frustrated by...

A desire I have, or a frustration I would like to shift, is...

An affirmation (or multiple) to describe my desired reality is...

I feel grateful for...

date: _____

Today, I feel energized by...

Today, I feel drained or frustrated by...

A desire I have, or a frustration I would like to shift, is...

An affirmation (or multiple) to describe my desired reality is...

I feel grateful for...

date: _____

Today, I feel energized by...

Today, I feel drained or frustrated by...

A desire I have, or a frustration I would like to shift, is...

An affirmation (or multiple) to describe my desired reality is...

I feel grateful for...

date: _____

Looking at the last few entries, what consistently energized or excited me? How can I made more space for those things in my life?

*What consistently drained me?
How could I minimize these activities?*

Have I had any negative thoughts or frustrations? How could I shift these thoughts to match the reality I want to create?

What changes have I noticed in my thinking or reality since I began reprogramming my mind?

this week, I felt energized...

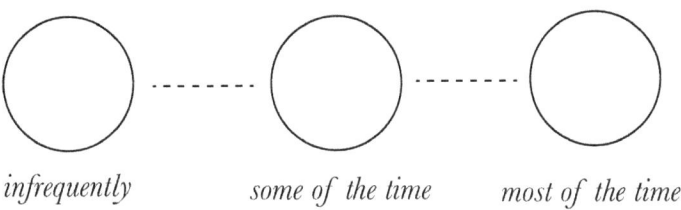

i felt positive about reaching my goals and making my dreams reality...

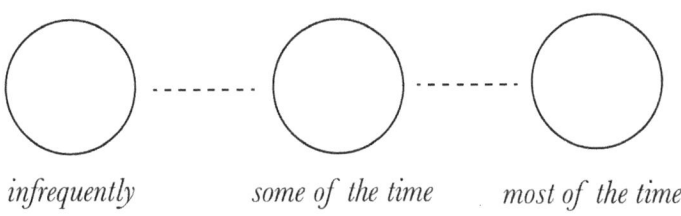

i felt magnetic, flowing, and satisfied...

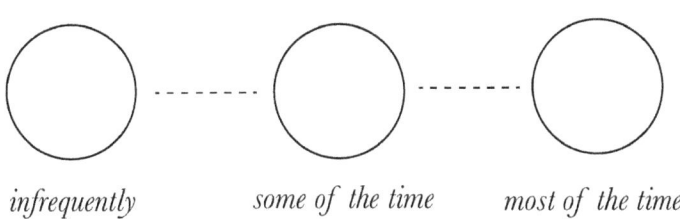

I can always shift my reality.

date: _____

Today, I feel energized by...

Today, I feel drained or frustrated by...

A desire I have, or a frustration I would like to shift, is...

An affirmation (or multiple) to describe my desired reality is...

I feel grateful for...

date: _____

Today, I feel energized by...

Today, I feel drained or frustrated by...

A desire I have, or a frustration I would like to shift, is...

An affirmation (or multiple) to describe my desired reality is...

I feel grateful for...

date: _____

Today, I feel energized by...

Today, I feel drained or frustrated by...

A desire I have, or a frustration I would like to shift, is...

An affirmation (or multiple) to describe my desired reality is...

I feel grateful for...

date: _____

Today, I feel energized by...

Today, I feel drained or frustrated by...

A desire I have, or a frustration I would like to shift, is...

An affirmation (or multiple) to describe my desired reality is...

I feel grateful for...

date: _____

Today, I feel energized by...

Today, I feel drained or frustrated by...

A desire I have, or a frustration I would like to shift, is...

An affirmation (or multiple) to describe my desired reality is...

I feel grateful for...

date: _____

Today, I feel energized by...

Today, I feel drained or frustrated by...

A desire I have, or a frustration I would like to shift, is...

An affirmation (or multiple) to describe my desired reality is...

I feel grateful for...

Everyone is different, and that is beautiful.

date: _____

Looking at the last few entries, what consistently energized or excited me? How can I made more space for those things in my life?

*What consistently drained me?
How could I minimize these activities?*

Have I had any negative thoughts or frustrations? How could I shift these thoughts to match the reality I want to create?

What changes have I noticed in my thinking or reality since I began reprogramming my mind?

this week, I felt energized...

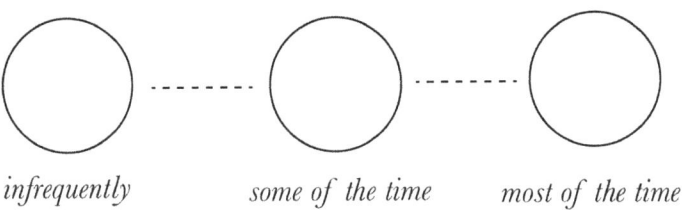

i felt positive about reaching my goals and making my dreams reality...

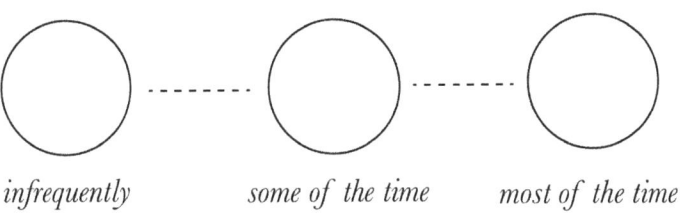

i felt magnetic, flowing, and satisfied...

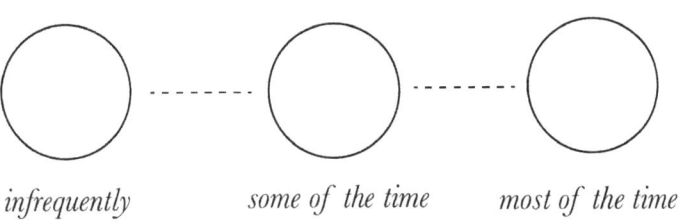

date: _____

Today, I feel energized by...

Today, I feel drained or frustrated by...

A desire I have, or a frustration I would like to shift, is...

An affirmation (or multiple) to describe my desired reality is...

I feel grateful for...

date: _____

Today, I feel energized by...

Today, I feel drained or frustrated by...

A desire I have, or a frustration I would like to shift, is...

An affirmation (or multiple) to describe my desired reality is...

I feel grateful for...

date: _____

Today, I feel energized by...

Today, I feel drained or frustrated by...

A desire I have, or a frustration I would like to shift, is...

An affirmation (or multiple) to describe my desired reality is...

I feel grateful for...

date: _____

Today, I feel energized by...

Today, I feel drained or frustrated by...

A desire I have, or a frustration I would like to shift, is...

An affirmation (or multiple) to describe my desired reality is...

I feel grateful for...

date: _____

Today, I feel energized by...

Today, I feel drained or frustrated by...

A desire I have, or a frustration I would like to shift, is...

An affirmation (or multiple) to describe my desired reality is...

I feel grateful for...

date: _____

Today, I feel energized by...

Today, I feel drained or frustrated by...

A desire I have, or a frustration I would like to shift, is...

An affirmation (or multiple) to describe my desired reality is...

I feel grateful for...

date: _____

Looking at the last few entries, what consistently energized or excited me? How can I made more space for those things in my life?

*What consistently drained me?
How could I minimize these activities?*

Have I had any negative thoughts or frustrations? How could I shift these thoughts to match the reality I want to create?

What changes have I noticed in my thinking or reality since I began reprogramming my mind?

this week, I felt energized...

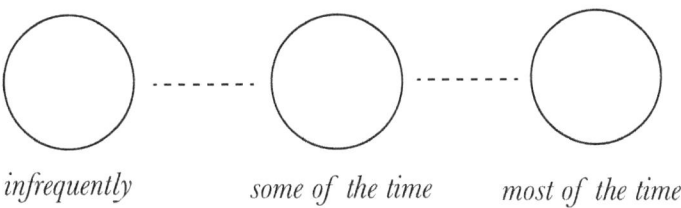

i felt positive about reaching my goals and making my dreams reality...

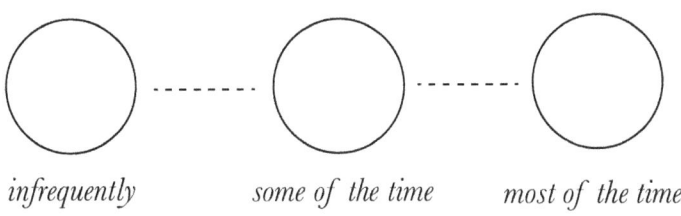

i felt magnetic, flowing, and satisfied...

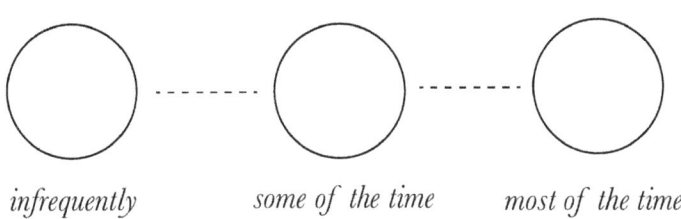

When I honor my
internal guidance,
the next steps
always appear.

date: _____

Today, I feel energized by...

Today, I feel drained or frustrated by...

A desire I have, or a frustration I would like to shift, is...

An affirmation (or multiple) to describe my desired reality is...

I feel grateful for...

date: _____

Today, I feel energized by...

Today, I feel drained or frustrated by...

A desire I have, or a frustration I would like to shift, is...

An affirmation (or multiple) to describe my desired reality is...

I feel grateful for...

date: _____

Today, I feel energized by...

Today, I feel drained or frustrated by...

A desire I have, or a frustration I would like to shift, is...

An affirmation (or multiple) to describe my desired reality is...

I feel grateful for...

date: _____

Today, I feel energized by...

Today, I feel drained or frustrated by...

A desire I have, or a frustration I would like to shift, is...

An affirmation (or multiple) to describe my desired reality is...

I feel grateful for...

date: _____

Today, I feel energized by...

Today, I feel drained or frustrated by...

A desire I have, or a frustration I would like to shift, is...

An affirmation (or multiple) to describe my desired reality is...

I feel grateful for...

date: _____

Today, I feel energized by...

Today, I feel drained or frustrated by...

A desire I have, or a frustration I would like to shift, is...

An affirmation (or multiple) to describe my desired reality is...

I feel grateful for...

date: _____

Looking at the last few entries, what consistently energized or excited me? How can I made more space for those things in my life?

What consistently drained me?
How could I minimize these activities?

Have I had any negative thoughts or frustrations? How could I shift these thoughts to match the reality I want to create?

What changes have I noticed in my thinking or reality since I began reprogramming my mind?

this week, I felt energized...

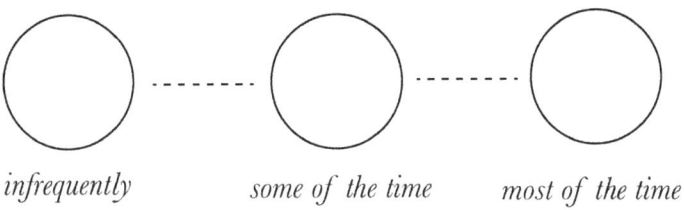

i felt positive about reaching my goals and making my dreams reality...

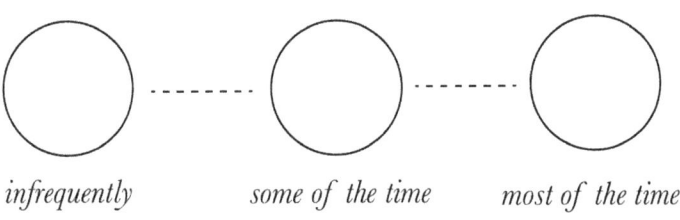

i felt magnetic, flowing, and satisfied...

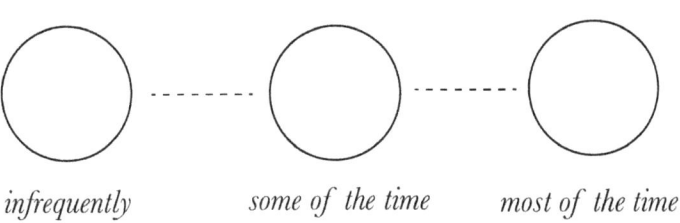

date: _____

Today, I feel energized by...

Today, I feel drained or frustrated by...

A desire I have, or a frustration I would like to shift, is...

An affirmation (or multiple) to describe my desired reality is...

I feel grateful for...

date: _____

Today, I feel energized by...

Today, I feel drained or frustrated by...

A desire I have, or a frustration I would like to shift, is...

An affirmation (or multiple) to describe my desired reality is...

I feel grateful for...

date: _____

Today, I feel energized by...

Today, I feel drained or frustrated by...

A desire I have, or a frustration I would like to shift, is...

An affirmation (or multiple) to describe my desired reality is...

I feel grateful for...

date: _____

Today, I feel energized by...

Today, I feel drained or frustrated by...

A desire I have, or a frustration I would like to shift, is...

An affirmation (or multiple) to describe my desired reality is...

I feel grateful for...

date: _____

Today, I feel energized by...

Today, I feel drained or frustrated by...

A desire I have, or a frustration I would like to shift, is...

An affirmation (or multiple) to describe my desired reality is...

I feel grateful for...

date: _____

Today, I feel energized by...

Today, I feel drained or frustrated by...

A desire I have, or a frustration I would like to shift, is...

An affirmation (or multiple) to describe my desired reality is...

I feel grateful for...

date: _____

Looking at the last few entries, what consistently energized or excited me? How can I made more space for those things in my life?

*What consistently drained me?
How could I minimize these activities?*

Have I had any negative thoughts or frustrations? How could I shift these thoughts to match the reality I want to create?

What changes have I noticed in my thinking or reality since I began reprogramming my mind?

this week, I felt energized...

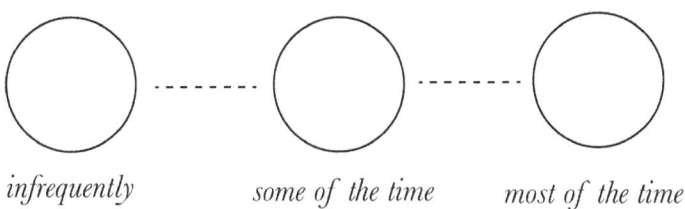

i felt positive about reaching my goals and making my dreams reality...

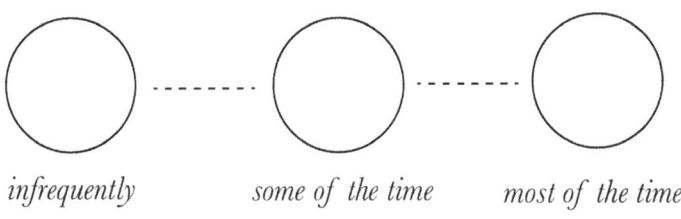

i felt magnetic, flowing, and satisfied...

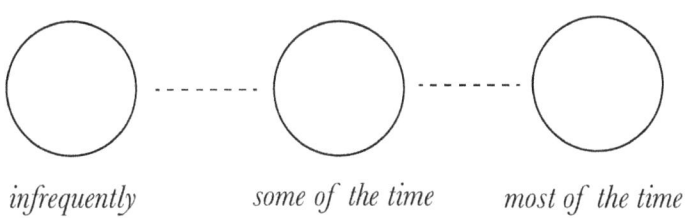

date:

Today, I feel energized by...

Today, I feel drained or frustrated by...

A desire I have, or a frustration I would like to shift, is...

An affirmation (or multiple) to describe my desired reality is...

I feel grateful for...

date: _____

Today, I feel energized by...

Today, I feel drained or frustrated by...

A desire I have, or a frustration I would like to shift, is...

An affirmation (or multiple) to describe my desired reality is...

I feel grateful for...

date: _____

Today, I feel energized by...

Today, I feel drained or frustrated by...

A desire I have, or a frustration I would like to shift, is...

An affirmation (or multiple) to describe my desired reality is...

I feel grateful for...

date: _____

Today, I feel energized by...

Today, I feel drained or frustrated by...

A desire I have, or a frustration I would like to shift, is...

An affirmation (or multiple) to describe my desired reality is...

I feel grateful for...

date: _____

Today, I feel energized by...

Today, I feel drained or frustrated by...

A desire I have, or a frustration I would like to shift, is...

An affirmation (or multiple) to describe my desired reality is...

I feel grateful for...

date: _____

Today, I feel energized by...

Today, I feel drained or frustrated by...

A desire I have, or a frustration I would like to shift, is...

An affirmation (or multiple) to describe my desired reality is...

I feel grateful for...

Money flows effortlessly into my life.

date: _____

Looking at the last few entries, what consistently energized or excited me? How can I made more space for those things in my life?

*What consistently drained me?
How could I minimize these activities?*

Have I had any negative thoughts or frustrations? How could I shift these thoughts to match the reality I want to create?

What changes have I noticed in my thinking or reality since I began reprogramming my mind?

this week, I felt energized...

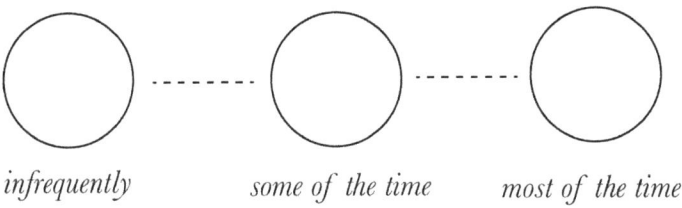

i felt positive about reaching my goals and making my dreams reality...

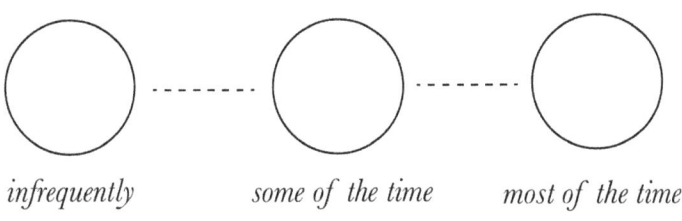

i felt magnetic, flowing, and satisfied...

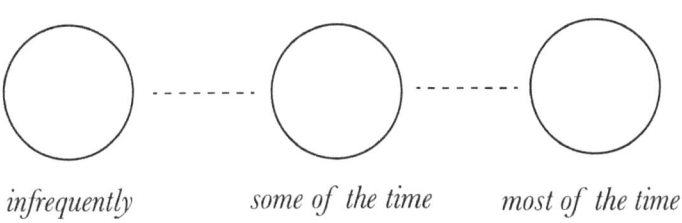

date: _____

Today, I feel energized by...

Today, I feel drained or frustrated by...

A desire I have, or a frustration I would like to shift, is...

An affirmation (or multiple) to describe my desired reality is...

I feel grateful for...

date: _____

Today, I feel energized by...

Today, I feel drained or frustrated by...

A desire I have, or a frustration I would like to shift, is...

An affirmation (or multiple) to describe my desired reality is...

I feel grateful for...

date: _____

Today, I feel energized by...

Today, I feel drained or frustrated by...

A desire I have, or a frustration I would like to shift, is...

An affirmation (or multiple) to describe my desired reality is...

I feel grateful for...

date: _____

Today, I feel energized by...

Today, I feel drained or frustrated by...

A desire I have, or a frustration I would like to shift, is...

An affirmation (or multiple) to describe my desired reality is...

I feel grateful for...

date: _____

Today, I feel energized by...

Today, I feel drained or frustrated by...

A desire I have, or a frustration I would like to shift, is...

An affirmation (or multiple) to describe my desired reality is...

I feel grateful for...

date: _____

Today, I feel energized by...

Today, I feel drained or frustrated by...

A desire I have, or a frustration I would like to shift, is...

An affirmation (or multiple) to describe my desired reality is...

I feel grateful for...

date: _____

Looking at the last few entries, what consistently energized or excited me? How can I made more space for those things in my life?

*What consistently drained me?
How could I minimize these activities?*

Have I had any negative thoughts or frustrations? How could I shift these thoughts to match the reality I want to create?

What changes have I noticed in my thinking or reality since I began reprogramming my mind?

this week, I felt energized...

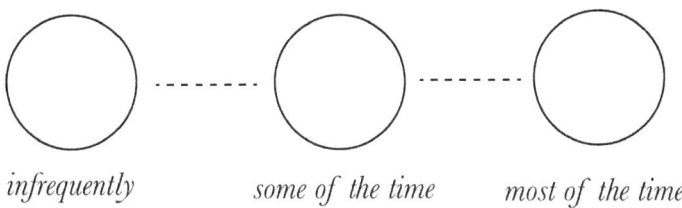

i felt positive about reaching my goals and making my dreams reality...

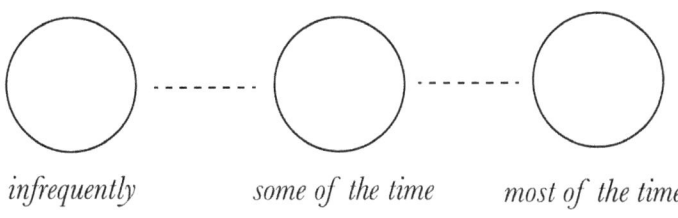

i felt magnetic, flowing, and satisfied...

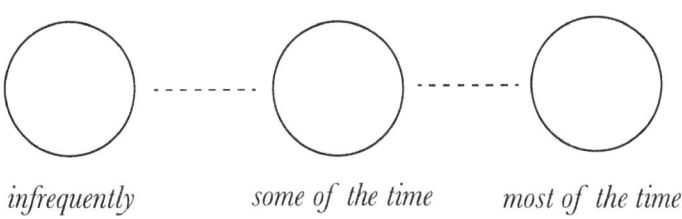

The planet supports my unique frequency.

date: _____

Today, I feel energized by...

Today, I feel drained or frustrated by...

A desire I have, or a frustration I would like to shift, is...

An affirmation (or multiple) to describe my desired reality is...

I feel grateful for...

date: _____

Today, I feel energized by...

Today, I feel drained or frustrated by...

A desire I have, or a frustration I would like to shift, is...

An affirmation (or multiple) to describe my desired reality is...

I feel grateful for...

date: _____

Today, I feel energized by...

Today, I feel drained or frustrated by...

A desire I have, or a frustration I would like to shift, is...

An affirmation (or multiple) to describe my desired reality is...

I feel grateful for...

date: _____

Today, I feel energized by...

Today, I feel drained or frustrated by...

A desire I have, or a frustration I would like to shift, is...

An affirmation (or multiple) to describe my desired reality is...

I feel grateful for...

date: _____

Today, I feel energized by...

Today, I feel drained or frustrated by...

A desire I have, or a frustration I would like to shift, is...

An affirmation (or multiple) to describe my desired reality is...

I feel grateful for...

date: _____

Today, I feel energized by...

Today, I feel drained or frustrated by...

A desire I have, or a frustration I would like to shift, is...

An affirmation (or multiple) to describe my desired reality is...

I feel grateful for...

I attract opportunities to respond to.

date: _____

Looking at the last few entries, what consistently energized or excited me? How can I made more space for those things in my life?

*What consistently drained me?
How could I minimize these activities?*

Have I had any negative thoughts or frustrations? How could I shift these thoughts to match the reality I want to create?

What changes have I noticed in my thinking or reality since I began reprogramming my mind?

this week, I felt energized...

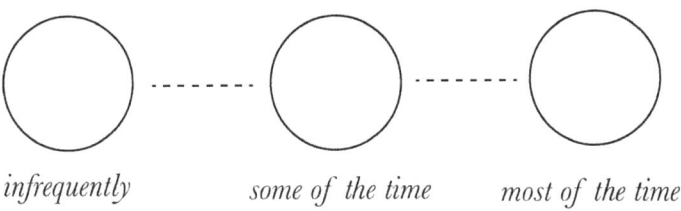

i felt positive about reaching my goals and making my dreams reality...

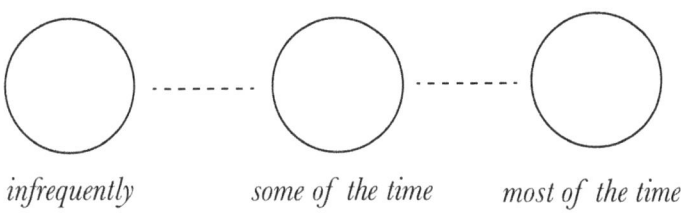

i felt magnetic, flowing, and satisfied...

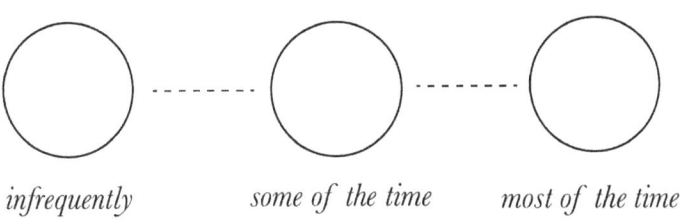

date: _____

Today, I feel energized by...

Today, I feel drained or frustrated by...

A desire I have, or a frustration I would like to shift, is...

An affirmation (or multiple) to describe my desired reality is...

I feel grateful for...

date: _____

Today, I feel energized by...

Today, I feel drained or frustrated by...

A desire I have, or a frustration I would like to shift, is...

An affirmation (or multiple) to describe my desired reality is...

I feel grateful for...

date: _____

Today, I feel energized by...

Today, I feel drained or frustrated by...

A desire I have, or a frustration I would like to shift, is...

An affirmation (or multiple) to describe my desired reality is...

I feel grateful for...

date: _____

Today, I feel energized by...

Today, I feel drained or frustrated by...

A desire I have, or a frustration I would like to shift, is...

An affirmation (or multiple) to describe my desired reality is...

I feel grateful for...

date: _____

Today, I feel energized by...

Today, I feel drained or frustrated by...

A desire I have, or a frustration I would like to shift, is...

An affirmation (or multiple) to describe my desired reality is...

I feel grateful for...

date: _____

Today, I feel energized by...

Today, I feel drained or frustrated by...

A desire I have, or a frustration I would like to shift, is...

An affirmation (or multiple) to describe my desired reality is...

I feel grateful for...

date: _____

Looking at the last few entries, what consistently energized or excited me? How can I made more space for those things in my life?

*What consistently drained me?
How could I minimize these activities?*

Have I had any negative thoughts or frustrations? How could I shift these thoughts to match the reality I want to create?

What changes have I noticed in my thinking or reality since I began reprogramming my mind?

this week, I felt energized...

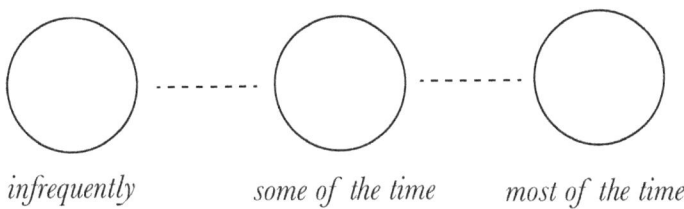

i felt positive about reaching my goals and making my dreams reality...

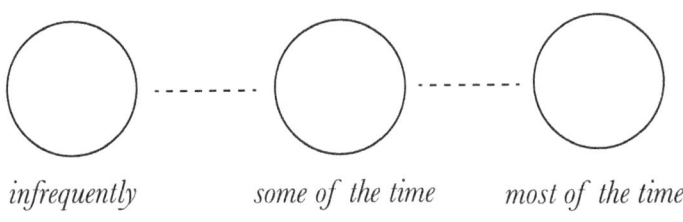

i felt magnetic, flowing, and satisfied...

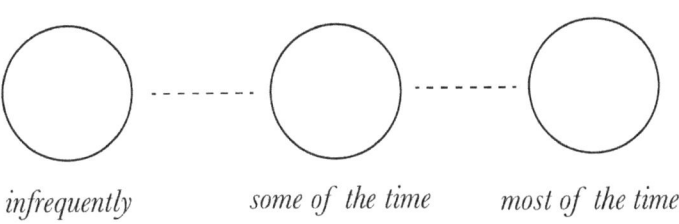

I
can
trust
my
life force
and where
it
leads
me

date:

Today, I feel energized by...

Today, I feel drained or frustrated by...

A desire I have, or a frustration I would like to shift, is...

An affirmation (or multiple) to describe my desired reality is...

I feel grateful for...

date: _____

Today, I feel energized by...

Today, I feel drained or frustrated by...

A desire I have, or a frustration I would like to shift, is...

An affirmation (or multiple) to describe my desired reality is...

I feel grateful for...

date: _____

Today, I feel energized by...

Today, I feel drained or frustrated by...

A desire I have, or a frustration I would like to shift, is...

An affirmation (or multiple) to describe my desired reality is...

I feel grateful for...

date: _____

Today, I feel energized by...

Today, I feel drained or frustrated by...

A desire I have, or a frustration I would like to shift, is...

An affirmation (or multiple) to describe my desired reality is...

I feel grateful for...

date: _____

Today, I feel energized by...

Today, I feel drained or frustrated by...

A desire I have, or a frustration I would like to shift, is...

An affirmation (or multiple) to describe my desired reality is...

I feel grateful for...

date: _____

Today, I feel energized by...

Today, I feel drained or frustrated by...

A desire I have, or a frustration I would like to shift, is...

An affirmation (or multiple) to describe my desired reality is...

I feel grateful for...

I am willing to do things that energize me.

date: _____

Looking at the last few entries, what consistently energized or excited me? How can I made more space for those things in my life?

*What consistently drained me?
How could I minimize these activities?*

Have I had any negative thoughts or frustrations? How could I shift these thoughts to match the reality I want to create?

What changes have I noticed in my thinking or reality since I began reprogramming my mind?

this week, I felt energized...

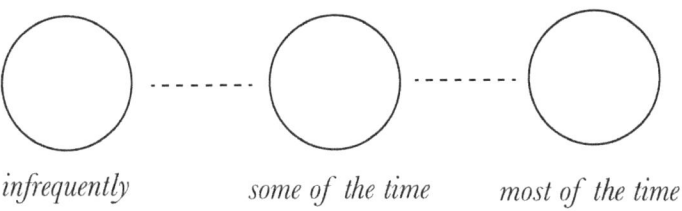

i felt positive about reaching my goals and making my dreams reality...

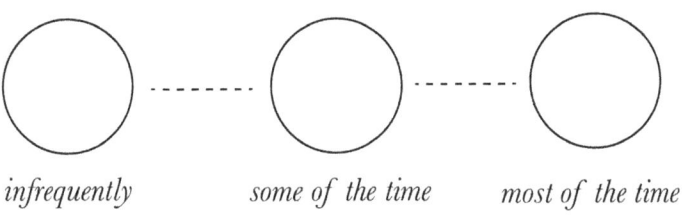

i felt magnetic, flowing, and satisfied...

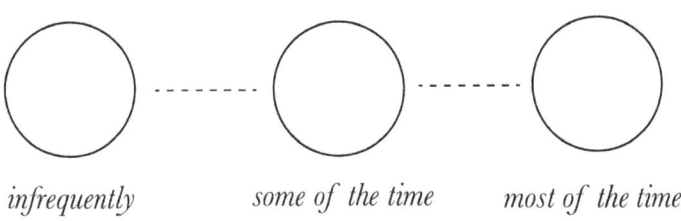

date: _____

Today, I feel energized by...

Today, I feel drained or frustrated by...

A desire I have, or a frustration I would like to shift, is...

An affirmation (or multiple) to describe my desired reality is...

I feel grateful for...

date: _____

Today, I feel energized by...

Today, I feel drained or frustrated by...

A desire I have, or a frustration I would like to shift, is...

An affirmation (or multiple) to describe my desired reality is...

I feel grateful for...

date: _____

Today, I feel energized by...

Today, I feel drained or frustrated by...

A desire I have, or a frustration I would like to shift, is...

An affirmation (or multiple) to describe my desired reality is...

I feel grateful for...

date: _____

Today, I feel energized by...

Today, I feel drained or frustrated by...

A desire I have, or a frustration I would like to shift, is...

An affirmation (or multiple) to describe my desired reality is...

I feel grateful for...

date: _____

Today, I feel energized by...

Today, I feel drained or frustrated by...

A desire I have, or a frustration I would like to shift, is...

An affirmation (or multiple) to describe my desired reality is...

I feel grateful for...

date: _____

Today, I feel energized by...

Today, I feel drained or frustrated by...

A desire I have, or a frustration I would like to shift, is...

An affirmation (or multiple) to describe my desired reality is...

I feel grateful for...

date: _____

Looking at the last few entries, what consistently energized or excited me? How can I made more space for those things in my life?

*What consistently drained me?
How could I minimize these activities?*

Have I had any negative thoughts or frustrations? How could I shift these thoughts to match the reality I want to create?

What changes have I noticed in my thinking or reality since I began reprogramming my mind?

this week, I felt energized...

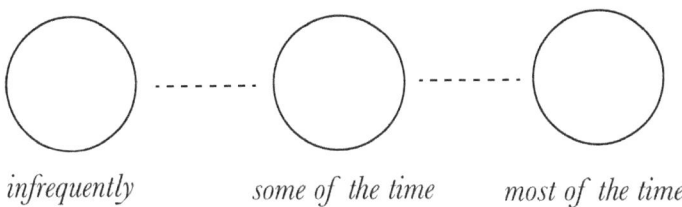

i felt positive about reaching my goals and making my dreams reality...

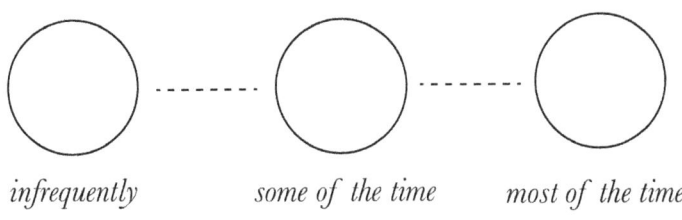

i felt magnetic, flowing, and satisfied...

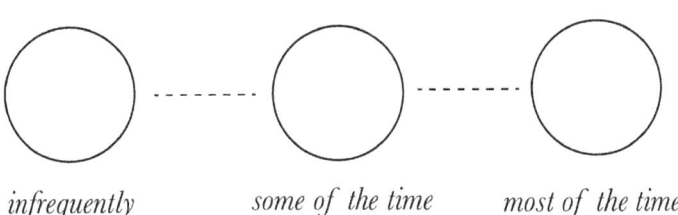

I deserve to get paid to do what I love.

date: _____

Today, I feel energized by...

Today, I feel drained or frustrated by...

A desire I have, or a frustration I would like to shift, is...

An affirmation (or multiple) to describe my desired reality is...

I feel grateful for...

date: _____

Today, I feel energized by...

Today, I feel drained or frustrated by...

A desire I have, or a frustration I would like to shift, is...

An affirmation (or multiple) to describe my desired reality is...

I feel grateful for...

date: _____

Today, I feel energized by...

Today, I feel drained or frustrated by...

A desire I have, or a frustration I would like to shift, is...

An affirmation (or multiple) to describe my desired reality is...

I feel grateful for...

date: _____

Today, I feel energized by...

Today, I feel drained or frustrated by...

A desire I have, or a frustration I would like to shift, is...

An affirmation (or multiple) to describe my desired reality is...

I feel grateful for...

date: _____

Today, I feel energized by...

Today, I feel drained or frustrated by...

A desire I have, or a frustration I would like to shift, is...

An affirmation (or multiple) to describe my desired reality is...

I feel grateful for...

date: _____

Today, I feel energized by...

Today, I feel drained or frustrated by...

A desire I have, or a frustration I would like to shift, is...

An affirmation (or multiple) to describe my desired reality is...

I feel grateful for...

I have a magnetic aura.

date: _____

Looking at the last few entries, what consistently energized or excited me? How can I made more space for those things in my life?

*What consistently drained me?
How could I minimize these activities?*

Have I had any negative thoughts or frustrations? How could I shift these thoughts to match the reality I want to create?

What changes have I noticed in my thinking or reality since I began reprogramming my mind?

this week, I felt energized...

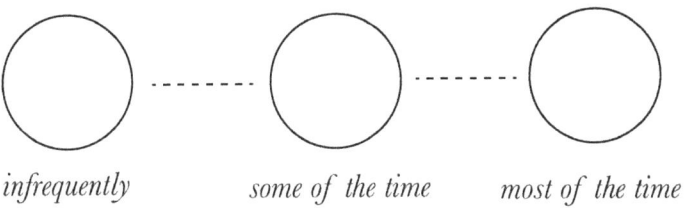

i felt positive about reaching my goals and making my dreams reality...

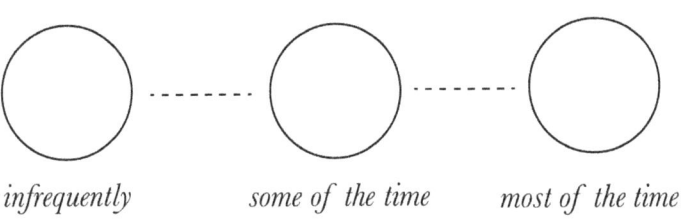

i felt magnetic, flowing, and satisfied...

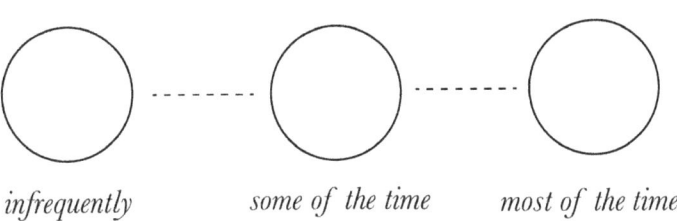

date: _____

Today, I feel energized by...

Today, I feel drained or frustrated by...

A desire I have, or a frustration I would like to shift, is...

An affirmation (or multiple) to describe my desired reality is...

I feel grateful for...

date: _____

Today, I feel energized by...

Today, I feel drained or frustrated by...

A desire I have, or a frustration I would like to shift, is...

An affirmation (or multiple) to describe my desired reality is...

I feel grateful for...

date: _____

Today, I feel energized by...

Today, I feel drained or frustrated by...

A desire I have, or a frustration I would like to shift, is...

An affirmation (or multiple) to describe my desired reality is...

I feel grateful for...

date: _____

Today, I feel energized by...

Today, I feel drained or frustrated by...

A desire I have, or a frustration I would like to shift, is...

An affirmation (or multiple) to describe my desired reality is...

I feel grateful for...

date: _____

Today, I feel energized by...

Today, I feel drained or frustrated by...

A desire I have, or a frustration I would like to shift, is...

An affirmation (or multiple) to describe my desired reality is...

I feel grateful for...

date: _____

Today, I feel energized by...

Today, I feel drained or frustrated by...

A desire I have, or a frustration I would like to shift, is...

An affirmation (or multiple) to describe my desired reality is...

I feel grateful for...

date: _____

Looking at the last few entries, what consistently energized or excited me? How can I made more space for those things in my life?

*What consistently drained me?
How could I minimize these activities?*

Have I had any negative thoughts or frustrations? How could I shift these thoughts to match the reality I want to create?

What changes have I noticed in my thinking or reality since I began reprogramming my mind?

this week, I felt energized...

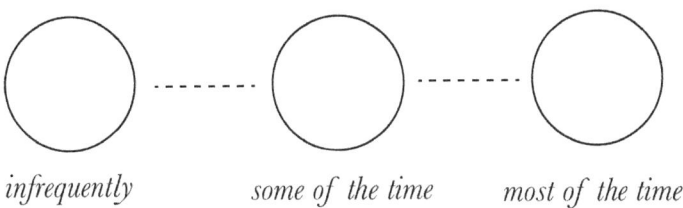

i felt positive about reaching my goals and making my dreams reality...

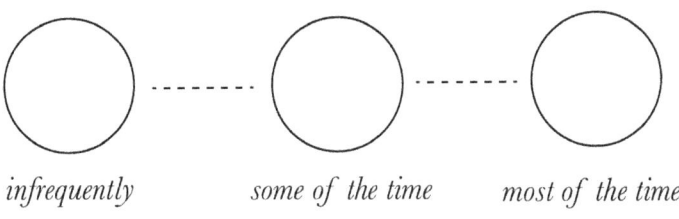

i felt magnetic, flowing, and satisfied...

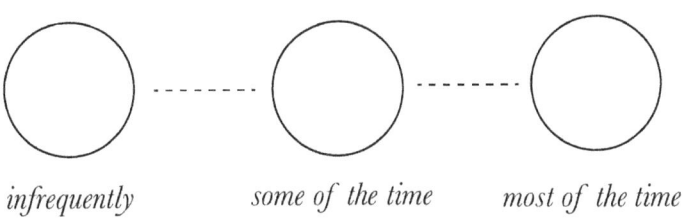

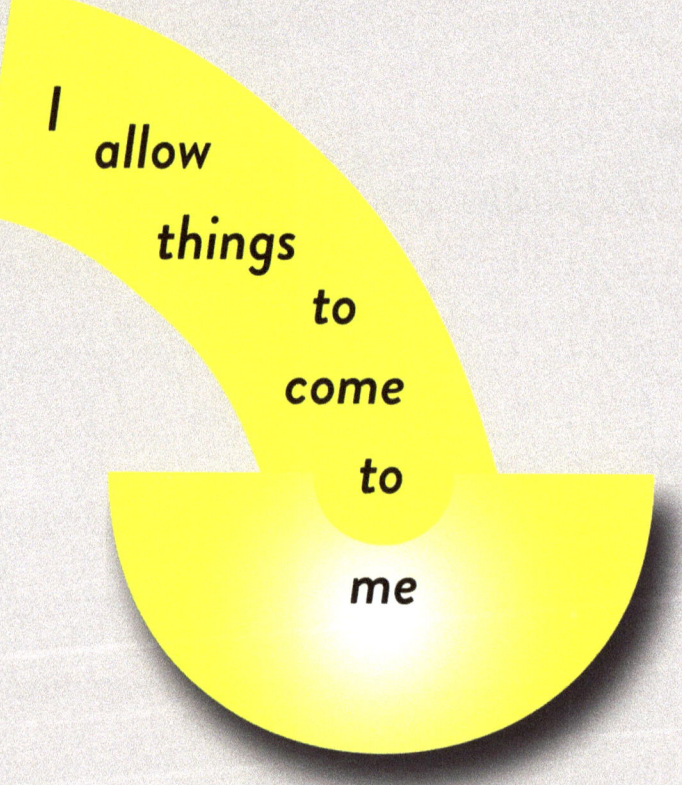

I am creating my reality.

I am creating my reality.

www.ingramcontent.com/pod-product-compliance
Lightning Source LLC
Chambersburg PA
CBHW060441281224
19562CB00048B/1797